W0115297

Five Seasons of a Golden Year
A Chinese Pastoral

RENDITIONS BOOKS

are issued by
the Comparative Literature and Translation Centre
The Chinese University of Hong Kong
publisher of *Renditions*,
a Chinese-English Translation Magazine

General Editors

Stephen C. Soong
George Kao

Fan Ch'eng-ta

Five Seasons of a Golden Year
A Chinese Pastoral

Translated by Gerald Bullett

Calligraphy by T. C. Lai

A *RENDITIONS* Book

The Chinese University Press
Hong Kong

International Standard Book Number:
962-201-246-9

Distributed by
The University of Washington Press
Seattle and London

Typesetting by Goldwind Photo Typesetting Co., Hong Kong
Printed by Winson Printing Company, Hong Kong

ACKNOWLEDGEMENTS

This book was originally published in England in 1946 under the title *The Golden Year of Fan Ch'eng-ta* by the Cambridge University Press. We are deeply grateful to Mrs. Rosalind Bullett for her kind permission to reproduce her late husband's work, presented here in a new format and in parallel Chinese and English texts. Our thanks are due to Mr. T. C. Lai, author of numerous books on things Chinese, who has embellished these pages with his calligraphy. The paintings preceding the five sections of this book, from a landscape album by Li Jan (1747-1799), are by courtesy of the Art Gallery of The Chinese University of Hong Kong. Mrs. Pansy Wong of The Chinese University Press has rendered invaluable help in the design of the book.

范成大

四時田園雜興六十首

CONTENTS

FAN CH'ENG-TA, author of the sequence
of poems here for the first time offered in
an English rendering, lived and died in our
twelfth century, that is, during the middle
years of the Sung dynasty. Like so many
other Chinese poets, he spent much of his
life in the state service, having in A.D. 1154
passed the highest literary examination and
become thereby an 'advanced scholar'. He
was born in 1126 and died in 1193, and he
is believed to have written these particular
poems during his sixtieth year, a year of
rural retirement from official life because
of failing health. His talents were both
military and diplomatic. By firmness and
shrewd strategy he succeeded in quelling
border rebellions, during his term of office
as military governor of Ssuchuan; and in an
earlier year he had greatly distinguished
himself in a diplomatic mission to the
court of a victorious ex-enemy, the Prince
of the Golden Race. As governor he made
a point of collecting poets round him and
using them on his staff. 'He employed them
to the best advantage', remarks a Chinese
historian, 'overlooking their small faults'.
One of these, Yang Wan-li, has left a tribute

both personal and literary: 'He surpasses all other contemporary poets. Myself, need I be too modest about my own poetry? But to him I bow my head. In conversation, whether on the newest and most curious subjects or on the highest philosophical abstractions, he was no less a master than were the scholars of the Tsin-Sung period. As for his poems, when the work is weighty it has the force of a river in flood, and when it is in miniature form it has the delicate modelling of an ear of corn, rich without excess, precise without tenuity.' We are told, further, that Governor Fan's administration in Ssuchuan was exceptionally wise, benevolent, and fruitful of good to all classes of the people, from the peasants, whom he cared for in times of difficulty, to the army, whose generals he chose with great shrewdness (for their poetical talent, one hopes) and whose equipment he studied to improve; and that whenever he wrote a poem, in the abundant leisure he enjoyed after masterfully solving these official problems, no sooner was the ink dry upon the paper than 'tens of thousands of men and women were copying and reading it. Calligraphers would write it on silk screens or on fans, and give

them to their friends.' One is hardly sur-
prised to learn that no previous governor
of Ssuchuan had been so honoured.

My part in the present undertaking is
dedicated, without his permission, to a
distinguished historian of Chinese civiliza-
tion, my friend Mr Ts'ui Chi, who with
untiring kindness opened for me the eight-
and-twenty doors into each of the sixty
poems here translated. Read as a continu-
ing sequence they present a poet's picture
of rural life in the district of Soochow eight
centuries ago. Each in the original consists
of four, end-stopped, seven-word lines,
rhymed *a a b a* or *a b c b*. Classical Chinese
being an extremely allusive and an extreme-
ly condensed language, and the peculiar
music of Chinese poetry being strictly
inimitable in English, a translator into
English verse has no alternative but to find
a form of his own. When Ts'ui Chi had
supplied me with literal equivalents (where
they could be found) of the twenty-eight
words in each poem, I found that for me
the best plan was to render each long
Chinese line in two not so long English
ones; and taking a middle way between
formalism and freedom I have used half-
rhyme and other coupling devices, as well

as full rhyme. My immersion in the mind of a twelfth-century Chinese poet during the midsummer weeks of this year has been a rich experience, of which some part, I hope, may be shared with the reader of the following pages.

G. B.

AUTUMN 1945

AN EXPERIMENT IN TRANSLATION

梅 子 金 黄 杏 子 肥

Heavy the trees with load of golden plum,
To mellow age the almond fruit is come . . .

It was early in June, a few weeks after victory had been won in Europe, that my Chinese friend Ts'ui Chi came for a three days' stay with me in Sussex. We had become acquainted two or three years earlier, so that I had had plenty of time to discover that he was really and truly Chinese: by which I mean not merely a member of the Chinese race but one who, with all his knowledge of English and his mastery of western ideas, embodied in his person and philosophy the spirit of all that is most vital in the ancient Chinese culture. Though he had spent some years in England, and had written in English a short history of

Chinese civilization, he still looked out upon the world through Chinese eyes.

An Anglo-Chinese friendship is in itself no matter for wonder. The two peoples, with all their obvious differences of tradition and outlook, have (or had, in 1945) at least two or three very important things in common. They enjoy the same kind of humour; they both have a native sense of irony; they value highly the simple pleasures and affections of everyday life; and they are keenly alive to the beauties and enchantment of the natural scene. In Chinese poetry some of the most delightful effects are achieved by a simple (but subtle) matter-of-factness or by delicate understatement, both qualities highly congenial to a cultivated—and often to an uncultivated—English taste. Our friendship, therefore, was in no way surprising: what was surprising, and for me extraordinarily lucky, was that Ts'ui Chi brought with him, in his pocket, my passport not merely into a remote time and place but into another and a serenely luminous mind.

He spoke of it, shyly, tentatively, within an hour of his arrival, while we were walking together at the foot of the downs. "I've brought a few poems," he said. "I thought you might like to try turning them into English." And, when we got back to the house, after a little encouragement he fished out a note-book into which he had copied, in the Chinese character, a sequence of no fewer than sixty small poems celebrating the rural year, twelve for each of five seasons. Their author, Fan Ch'eng-ta, had lived and died in our twelfth century: that is, during the middle years of the Sung dynasty. Like so many other Chinese poets, he spent much of his life in the State service, having in A.D. 1154 passed the highest literary examination and become thereby an "advanced scholar." He was born in 1126 and died in 1193, and he is believed to have written these particular poems during his sixtieth year, a year of rural retirement from official life because of failing health. He is not, apparently, among the best-known of Chinese poets. Nothing of his had ever been translated into English before; Mr. Arthur Waley, to whom most of us owe what little acquaintance we have with Chinese poetry, has never had occasion to mention him in print; and one might reasonably have supposed that the gentlemen of the Press who were to review my English version had never heard of him—any more than I myself had, until Ts'ui Chi instructed me. How surprising therefore, and how gratifying, to find one or two among them retailing to their readers, with a most convincing air of lifelong familiarity with the subject, the facts supplied in my preface! One reviewer went further. We had been rash enough to have the first line of each section printed in Chinese as a decorative headline; and, pouncing upon the first of these, our critic complained that the first couplet of the first poem:

柳 花 深 巷 午 雞 聲

But for the cockerel calling the noon hour,
No voice is heard in the lane of willow-flower

was an inaccurate rendering of the original. The word *shen*, he asserted, meant *deep*; the proper translation would have been *deep lane*; and he implied that there was nothing in the Chinese text corresponding

xvi

to "No voice is heard."

I quote this Cambridge reviewer, not to invite admiration of his sublime persuasion that he understands the subtleties of Chinese poetry better than a Chinese specialist in the subject (who had of course carefully vetted my version), but because Ts'ui Chi's answer does incidentally throw some light on the nature of that most remote (from ours) of all civilized languages. The word *shen* does not necessarily mean *deep*. It can just as well be interpreted as *deadly quiet*. As objects sink deep under water, so may voices sink and vanish from the air. The noon-time, the cockerel's call, the drifting of willow catkins, point not only in fact, but also (said Ts'ui Chi) in the traditional poetical language, to a quiet scene. Moreover, a country lane is not generally a "deep" one, nor a long lane necessarily a quiet place. Finally, the expression *lu hsiang*, which occurs in the line in question, often suggests voices: therefore "No voice is heard in the lane of willow-flower" is a legitimate, and indeed a true, rendering.

This part of Ts'ui's answer to our critic did not reach print: it was omitted for lack of space. The part that *was* printed, however, contains so illuminating an exposition of the method used by Fan Ch'eng-ta that it must not be allowed to remain buried alive in the files of a university journal. The reviewer, writes Ts'ui Chi,

seems to have fallen into the popular error of supposing that all Chinese poems are as much "condensed" in spirit and meaning as in form, and that such a line as *almond golden yellow plum plump* would therefore be an "accurate" rendering. But that is not so. The various forms of poetry, under the general category *Ku Feng* (the Ancient Air), are longer and freer poems than the four-line and eight-line poetry developed later. These forms of poetry, called *chüeh chü*, had been first developed in the fourth or the sixth century, and remain in use up till the present time. The great length of its history and the shortness of its form have led to the development of a poetical diction and a special technique of grammatical arrangement, by which more ideas may be expressed than the words actually represent. The Chinese poets adore an arrangement by which "the idea exists beyond words." The method is peculiarly Chinese; it cannot be imitated in another language and it is effective only for readers who understand the *chüeh chü* tradition well. There are words, for instance, in a poem, called the "eyes," which by means of subtle arrangement are made to suggest more meanings and ideas, and to convey a richer picture to the mind's eye, than they would ordinarily do. Such an art the Chinese call "to forge" or "to refine." In translation it cannot be reproduced, because the key-word, which in the original suggests more ideas than the one commonly associated with it, can have no exact counterpart in another language which has necessarily a different literary tradition. The Chinese poet writes, but does not think, in this "condensed" style. Therefore, to be fair to him, in translating him we must seem to amplify.

Read as a continuing sequence, these sixty *chüeh chü* poems of Fan Ch'eng-ta, of which I was to attempt to produce English verse-renderings, present a poet's picture of rural life in the district of Soochow eight centuries ago. Each in the original consists of four, end-stopped, seven-word lines, rhymed *a a b a* or *a b c b*; and it must be remembered that in Chinese every word is a fixed monosyllable whose relation to its context is determined by position, by literary atmosphere and association, and by heaven knows what—never by inflexion. Chinese is an entirely uninflected language, and its poetry, though far from disdaining statement, consists not in the thing stated (though that is a contributory element) but in the scent and colour, the nimbus of suggestion and even of conjecture, arising out of the particular choice and arrangement of ideographs.

My attempt at the first poem of the series meeting with Ts'ui Chi's approval, we settled down to systematic work. I produced (appropriately enough) a school exercise-book; I divided my pages into seven columns, one for each word of each line; and off we went, I writing down the English literal equivalents (where they could be found) at Ts'ui Chi's dictation. "First line. First word: soil or earth. Second word: fertile, cream, fat, or grease. Third word: intend or wish. Fourth word: move or develop. Fifth word: rain. Sixth word: frequently. Seventh word: urge, press, or encourage. First word of second line: ten thousand. Second word: grasses or herb"—and so on. This was one of the easier ones. When we reached the last word of the last (fourth) line, my instructor, in a few words, would give me the general sense and feeling of the stanz (or poem) as a whole. I was thus put into possession not only of the twenty-eight nearest equivalents but of as many explanatory meanings as possible, particularly of the "eyes" or key-words; for, as has been said, in each poem there are ideas "off the poem" (in Ts'ui Chi's phrase) but suggested by it.

Without these final expositions my copious notes would clearly have been useless to me; but the expositions would themselves have been useless, and fruitless, had I not been enabled by them to enter imaginatively into the mind of the poet and enjoy for myself, at however distant a remove, the imaginative experience which had inspired the original. Whatever the shortcomings of the resulting English poems, the writing of them was a peculiarly rich experience precisely because it involved my immersion, for hours at a time, in the mind of that twelfth-century Chinese poet, when, after Ts'ui Chi had returned to

London leaving me with my garnered store of literal and associated meanings, it was my task to re-live, re-create, and record in my own fashion but with the utmost possible fidelity to the original imagery (since that was of the essence of the matter), each one of sixty separate consecutive small poems. A celestial task, arduous but infinitely fascinating! The sense (the illusion if you like) of being in intimate touch with a remote yet still living past provided the perfect escape, not only from a world that is always too much with us, but from my very self. Self-oblivion, the sages have said, is the only path to paradise; and it seems improbable that I shall ever again, in this uneasy world, be granted three midsummer weeks at once as exciting and serene as those I enjoyed in 1945.

This article originally appeared in the August 1954 issue of *Literary Guide*, a London publication. Gerald William Bullett, English poet and critic, was editor of *The English Galaxy of Shorter Poems* (1939) and *Silver Poets of the Sixteenth Century* (1947), both published in the Everyman's Library. His collaborator in the translation of the poems of Fan Ch'eng-ta, Ts'ui Chi (崔驥), was the author of *A Short History of Chinese Civilization* (1943), New York: G. P. Putnam's Sons.

春日

Early Spring

柳花深巷午雞聲

柳花深巷午雞聲
桑葉尖新綠未成
坐睡覺來無一事
滿窗晴日看蠶生

*B*ut for the cockerel calling the noon
hour,
No voice is heard in the lane of willow-
flower.
The young leaves of the mulberry, half-
uncurl'd,
Are showing their green tips to the warm
world.
Waking from quiet dreams, where I drowse
in my chair,
With nothing to do but enjoy the bright air,
I look from my window, flooded now with
noon,
And see the silkworm break from her co-
coon.

土膏欲動雨頻催
萬草千花一餉開
舍後荒畦猶綠秀
鄰家鞭筍過牆來

*U*nder the silver lash of the small rain,
The quicken'd earth is bringing forth again:
Ten thousand spears of grass and sudden
    flowers
Spring up to meet the showers.
Behind the house the unweeded small
    demesne
Shows a patchwork pattern of varying
    green,
And from the neighbouring garden bamboo-
    roots
Creeping under the wall send up new
    shoots.

高田二麥接山青
傍水低田綠未耕
桃杏滿村春似錦
踏歌椎鼓過清明

3

*I*n the high fields the green of the wheat
    runs
To join the mountain curve, green and
    bronze.
The river meadows, not yet under plow,
A darker, more luxuriant, greenness show.
The village, aglow with flowering almond
    and peach,
Looks like a picture drawn with silver
    stitch:
And there the people, with song, dancing,
    and drum,
Make festival because the spring is come.

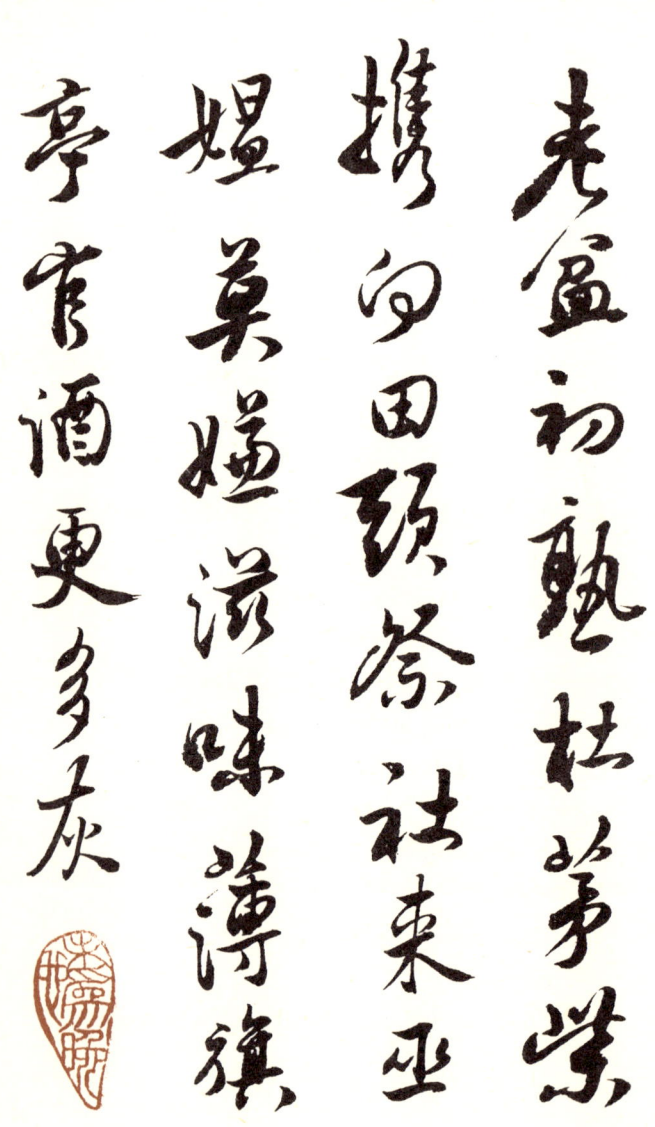

老盆初熟枇杷紫
攜向田頭餉社東巫
煜莫煻滋味薄旗
亭官酒更多灰

4

*N*ow to the field-shrine, from home
and hearth

We bring our offerings to the spirits of
earth,

Faggots and rushes, a dedicated hoard,

And food in an ancient vessel newly
prepared.

Whatever, O Priestess, the lifted lid disclose,

Don't wrinkle, Reverend One, your aged
nose:

Though you find the food insipid it's not
so thin

As the ritual wine you'll get at the village
inn.

社下燒錢鼓似雷日斜扶

得醉翁回青枝滿地花

狼藉知是兒孫鬭草來

5

*A*fter the festival of the burning of
cash,
The drums a diminishing thunder, the paper
ash,
At sundown the old man, having taken a
drop,
Goes zigzag homewards, on a friendly prop.
Strewn on the grass, flowers and leafy
boughs
Lie listless, as the serene air allows:
And he recalls, seeing the disarray,
That children have been here at play.

驕吟東來里巷喧
行春車馬鬧如煙
繫牛莫礙門前路
移繫門西碌碡邊

6

*T*rumpeted rumour of horsemen from
the east

Fills every lane and field with clamour of
feast.

The villagers swarm and stare,

Agog to see the galloping hosts appear.

And when, like a bright cloud, on noiseless
hooves

Into one's far vision the procession moves

—

Look, neighbour, to your cow! She's in the
way.

Tie her west of the gate, where she can't
stray.

空食花枝插滿頭
舊識青衫幾扁舟
一年一度遊山寺
不上靈巖即虎丘

7

*N*ow is the salad festival of spring,
When girls go revelling.
With flowers fresh, this morning of the year,
They skirt their limbs and cover their dark
    hair.
Flower-laden, under a clear sky,
The boats go by,
Either Ling Yen being the end in view,
Or the wide panorama of Hu Ch'iu.

郭裏人家拜掃回新開硬酒蒭青梅日長路好誠門近借我茅亭暖一杯

8

*A*fter the ritual sweeping of the tomb
The families from the city turn for home,
Having for tribute given the untasted jar
Of green-plum wine to the dead ancestor.
Long is the day and the road beautiful
That leads at last to the gate of the old wall.
Here in this arbour, under a friendly thatch,
We warm the wine and set a cup for each.

19

步屧尋春有好懷，雨餘歸道水如杯。随人黄犬擁前去，走入孔溪遂自迴。

9

*T*he rain over, I put my sandals on,
To walk where earlier wayfarers have gone,
Whose horses' hooves, imprinting in the
    mud
These brimming winecups, mark their
    joyous road.
My dog, following at heel as he's bid,
Soon forgets his master and runs ahead,
Till reaching a broad brook he stands at
    check,
Then soberly, unbidden, ambles back.

種園得果庶償勞
不攷兒童鳥雀搔
已插棘針樊筍径
更鋪漁網盖櫻桃

Swink how we may, evenings or early
morn,
Our garden crops bring only a bare return.
The seeds once planted, set in careful rows,
Children and birds must be accounted foes.
Here is a needling thorn-hedge, finger-high;
Here young bamboos shoot up to greet the
sky.
Let's now, to trick these thieving friends of
ours,
Turn fishermen and net the cherry-flowers.

吉日初開種稻包
南山雷動雨連宵
今年不欠秧田水
新漲看看拍小橋

*T*oday, with lifting heart and bow'd
    back,
Of rice-seed we open the first sack.
The thunderquake, which puts an end to
    drouth
And draws a blind over the crested south,
Is filling the fields with water, drop by
    drop,
And all the signs foretell a decent crop.
See, there, how the wallowing tide
Slaps at the bridge's underside.

桑下春蔬綠滿畦

菘心青嫩芥薹肥

溪頭洗擇店頭賣

日暮裹鹽沽酒歸

*U*nder his mulberry tree the goodman
   grows
Spring vegetables in nicely measured rows,
Mustard, and chives, and cabbage green and
   lush,
Which in due season at the brook he'll wash,
And singling out the choicest specimens
Will carry them to market. There he spends
On salt and wine the money newly won,
And with them gets him home at set of sun.

晚春

昨日�^帆大通^浮^船^月
煙水望三山^恍^如^武夷山
如算意在南宫此兒
聞己酉此月六日重作於
方以四日還村莊達^叟^

Late Spring

紫青蓴菜卷衫香

榮青薷菜卷荷香

玉樹芳芽拔薤長

自擷溪毛充晚供

短蓬風雨宿橫塘

Close-folding lettuce, lotus-scented,
    green
With the satin bloom of faggots' lichen-
    stain,
Spring onions white as snow and smooth as
    jade,
And celery trimm'd with many a sprouting
    bud:
Of these good things, a pilgrim under sail,
I gather abundance for an evening meal,
And under my awning, here on Heng Tang,
Shelter from wind and rain the night long.

湖蓮舊蕩藕新翻

小小荷錢沒漲痕

斟酌梅天風浪緊

更從外水種蘆根

14

On the shores of a desolate region of
    lake and sky,
The new-dug ivory roots of lotus lie.
Green coins of water-lily, lying so still,
Persuade us half to forget the gradual swell.
Now is the plum season, gusty and quick,
With petals flying and fruit soon to pick.
Savouring the hour I mark where bulrush
    shoots
Come sidling up from long lateral roots.

蛺蝶雙雙入菜花

日長無客到田家

雞飛過籬犬吠竇

知有行商來買茶

15

*B*utterflies, sauntering lazily here and
　　there,
Enter the vegetable flowers pair by pair.
I bathe in the golden stream of the long
　　day,
Having in mind no guest will come my way.
But hark! A bark! And from over the
　　bamboo fence
There's a sudden scatter of silly fugitive
　　hens!
I spend no time wondering who it can be:
A merchant come to buy my leaves of tea.

俯視水滿綠蘋洲
上巳微寒懶出遊
薄暮蛙聲連曉鬧
今年田稻十分秋

16

*A*t the flood's edge, among green
duckweeds plashing,
The islet-dweller is doing her household
washing.
On this day of Shang Ch'ih a man must
roam,
Though chilly air may bid him stay at
home.
Twilight is falling. Frogs, the night long,
Keep up their harsh, sonorous, croaking
song:
Fair omen that in this fine year of rain
Our rice will yield ten portions of good
grain.

新綠園林曉氣涼

晨炊蠶出看移秧

百花飄盡桑麻小

夾路風來阿魏香

17

*G*arden trees, in the cool glow of dawn,
Put on new green to enjoy the new sun.
Breakfasting early I walk in paradise
And watch my boys transplant the seedling
    rice.
Ten thousand falling petals scatter my path:
Mulberry and hemp show yet but meagre
    growth.
At every sauntering turn a wanderer meets
Odour of spices borne on a light breeze.

三旬聲忌閑門中
郡曲都無少住涯
縱是晚晴風露下
柔桑時與螢聲相逢

*F*or thirty days, jealous of visitors,
The silkworm lives unseen, behind shut
    doors.
Even the nearest of neighbours will refrain
From making footprints in the dusty lane.
Only on golden mornings, when the breeze
Scarce stirs the dew that lingers in the trees,
They come together to gather the mulberry
    leaf,
With serious smile and conversation brief.

汙菜一稜水周圍歲
歲蝸廬沒半扉不
看菱青雛護岸小
舟撐取薅田歸

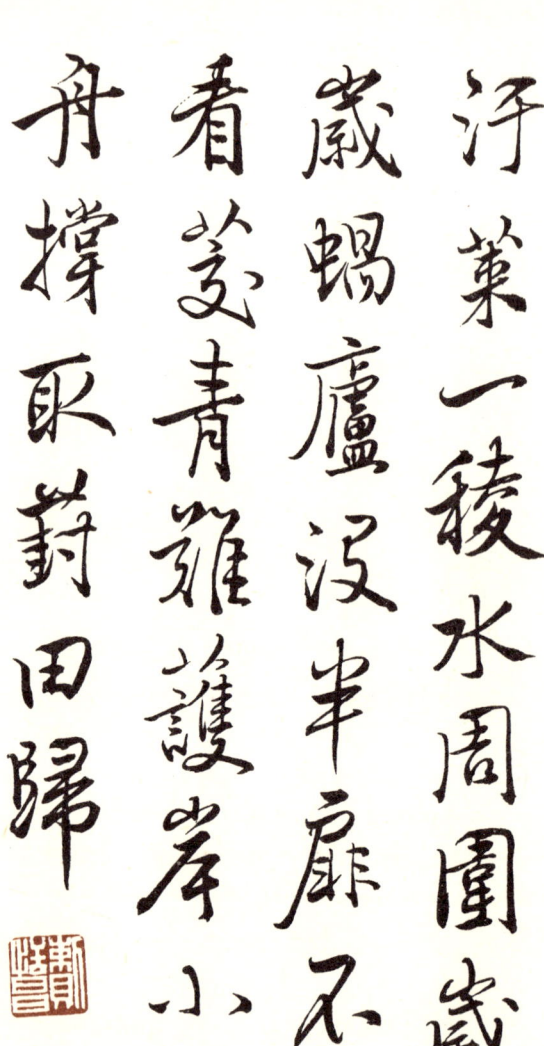

19

Today his plat of cultivated mud
Becomes an island sinking in the flood.
Today, from his snail-shell cottage, every
	year,
He sees the tidemark creeping up his door.
Did he not know by hard experience
The weakness of a planted water-fence,
Time and again he would have plied his oar
In search of rushes to defend the shore.

45

茅針香軟漸包萼
蓬檑甘酸半染紅
采采歸來兒女笑
扶頭高挂小篘籠

20

*H*ere downy, pointed reedlings,
   scabbard-bound,
In fragrant bundles wrap each other round.
Here russet berries somewhat wanly gleam,
Nature not having finished painting them.
Nevertheless, remembering my daughters
      and sons,
I find on the way plenty of likely ones;
And the children greet me gaily, seeing my
      pick
In the bamboo cage, at the end of my
      walking stick.

47

數雨如絲復似塵煮瓶

浮燼正脊新牡丹破蕚

櫻桃熟未許飛花減卻

春

21

*T*his day of the rice-in-husk festival,
The rain is silken, and perpetual.
The wax from my open'd bottle floats
    away;
I warm the wine and enjoy its fresh
    bouquet.
Peony blossoms from the calyx drop;
Already the cherry-tree carries a glowing
    crop.
These flying silks, these petals on the wing,
Cannot subdue today the spirit of spring.

雨後山家起較遲
天窗曉色半熹微
老翁欹枕聽鶯囀
童子開門放燕飛

*A*fter the rains, morning, airy and
    good,
Finds some of the country folk still in bed.
Here, the high window fills with dawn,
Of soft radiance, of dazzling sun.
This old one, roused by rustle and chirping
    calls,
Lies listening to the golden orioles.
The house boy, already up and about,
Opens the door to let a swallow out.

海雨江風浪作堆時
新魚業逐春回荻
芽抽笋汀鯰上棟子
閙花石首来

23

$\mathcal{A}$nd now, rivers rising and seas full,
Our world is water, with scarcely an
   interval.
Going in search of seasonable fish,
Soon we return with all that we could wish.
The sea-pig comes upstream; the edible
Miscanthus shoots are now ready to pull;
The oriental lilac blooms anew;
And the fish called Yellow Flower swims
   into view.

53

鳥鳥投林過客稀
山煙暝樹綠霏霏
一棹舟如葉狗自縮
闌鴨陣歸

24

*F*ew come this way, and if a stranger
    should,
See how the birds dart off, into the wood!
Shadows of dove-grey dusk the hills
    obscure,
And gathering reach my faggot-builded
    door.
In a boat light as a leaf, still visible,
My lad-of-all-work plies his single scull.
Alone, I weave my fence, of lithe bamboo,
And ducks go primly homewards, two by
    two.

夏
日

風雨如晦雞鳴不已以此花
榮代南宮泉二題

Summer

梅子金黄杏子肥

梅子金黃杏子肥

麥花雪白菜花稀

日長籬落無人過

惟有蜻蜓蛺蝶飛

25

*H*eavy the trees with load of golden
   plum,
To mellow age the almond fruit is come,
Flowers of the rape-turnip bloom and blow,
And the long barley blossoms into snow.
Long and serene my solitary day
Hedged in with summer and never a passer-
   by,
Except these bright-wing'd insect-travellers
Going about their glittering affairs.

五月江吳麥秀寒
移秧披絮尚衣單
稻根科斗行如塊
田水今年一尺寬

Soochow, in this fifth moon of the
   year,
Is cool as the cornfields come into ear.
Though padded their clothes with cotton
   stuff
The rice-field workers are scarcely warm
   enough.
Around the seedling roots, in a black
   swarm,
Innumerable tadpoles swim and squirm;
For the spring rains, in these fields of the
   rice crop,
Have covered the ground with water a foot
   deep.

乙麥俱秋斗百錢

田家喚作小豐年

餅爐飯瓶無飢色

接到西風熟稻天

27

*T*wo seasons' crops have yielded us so
    much,
A peck of corn brings only a hundred cash.
Even the peasant-farmers, many and poor,
Enjoy abundance this surprising year.
The oven's crammed with baking, and we
    know
Our cooking-pots assured of their modest
    due,
Till the golden western wind shall blow
    again,
To bring the season of ripening rice-grain.

百沸繰湯雪濺波

繅車嘈嘈雨鳴蓑

桑姑盆手文相賀

綿繭無多絲繭多

28

*C*ocoons, in boiling vats put to proof,
Thicken the rising water with snow-white
  surf.
The wheels of the spinning-cart buzz: the
  spray falls
Pat on the workers' dried-leaf overalls.
These mulberry-girls cross hands, as for a
  game,
To give each other joy of the great time,
Pleased that the coarser silk has proved to
  be rare
And the fine filament plentiful this year.

小婦連宵上絹機
大者催稅急於飛
今年幸甚蠶桑熟
苗得黃絲織夏衣

29

*D*ay after day the married daughters
   come,
To labour at the loom.
And year by year, swifter than dragonflies,
The tax-collectors swoop upon the prize.
This year, however, the mulberry and the
   worm
Have thrived together on even the smallest
   farm,
And the women are content with the
   yellow leavings
Allowed to them for their own weavings.

下田屝水出江流高壠
翻江遡上溝地勢不齊
人力畫丁男長立踏車
頤

From the low fields the water is
    forced up
To run with the river, and thence again to
    the top
To keep those watercourses flowing full
Which irrigate the highest fields of all.
These dispensations are the work of man,
No part of Nature's plan:
Upon this water-engine, age after age,
The feet of the young men tread with
    punctual pace.

71

畫出耘田夜績麻

村莊兒女各當家

童孫未解供耕織

也傍桑陰學種瓜

31

Sons in the fields all day, daughters at
    evening
Spinning hemp and weaving,
These with nimble fingers and strong arms
Contrive to keep things going on our farms.
This little grandchild, five years short of
    twelve,
As yet can neither spin nor deeply delve:
Yet even he, even so,
Under the mulberry his melon-seeds would
    grow.

槐葉初勻日氣涼
葱蒨鼠耳翠成雙
三公只得三株看
閒客清陰滿北窗

*M*ulberry, sophora, fair-grown and
    beautiful,
Hold themselves still, in air serenely cool.
The rhamnus grows in pairs, his leaves
    curl'd
Like rats' ears, his colour emerald.
Only the Three Dukes, the saying goes,
May look at the Three Trees.
Yet here, at his northern window, unafraid,
A simple man enjoys their benign shade.

黃塵行客汗如漿
少住儂家漱井香
借與門前磐石坐
柳陰亭午正風涼

33

Bedew'd with sweat and grimed with
    golden dust,
He lingers by the garden, an unknown
    guest,
Breaking a long journey to slake his drouth
With water from the well's fragrant mouth.
I lend my gate for him to lean upon,
And here's a millstone where he sits him
    down.
A freshet of wind in the willow-shaded air
Makes noontide cool, time an opening
    flower.

千頃芙蕖放棹嬉
花深迷路晚忘歸
家人暗識船行處
時有驚忙小鴨飛

34

In a many-acre field of lotus-flowers
I drift my boat and let loose my oars.
The way is hidden amid a mass of bloom,
And evening finds me still forgetful of
    home.
They who await me there know full well
My whereabouts, though seeing not my
    sail,
Whence, every now and again, into their
    sight,
Small waterfowls rise up, in sudden flight.

采薆辛苦慶犂鉏血
指流丹鬼質枯無力
買田聊種水近来湖
面点收租

35

*T*ime was he worked like others with
    plow and hoe,
But now a-gathering caltrops he must go:
Blood from his prickt fingers, trickling
    down,
Tinges the pale water vermilion.
Field who has none, nor any means to buy,
Must plant and reap in water, where he
    may:
And even then he can't hope to escape,
In these hard times, the tax-collectors' rape.

蜩螗千萬沸斜陽
蛙黽爭邊眠夜
長不把疵龍聲相對
治夢魂爭得到蔡
株

36

Shadows extend, under the slanting
    sun:
The cicadas' bubbling noise goes on and on.
The night falls, but frogs, too wide awake,
Cannot forbear their automatic croak.
Use now the art of being dull of sense,
And so by feigning find indifference:
How else may the dream-soul, each mortal
    has,
On viewless wing approach my bed of grass?

秋
日

芙蓉花時秋色妍映水裳紫玉煙何人
蒲水臨吟詠花裏歌聲樓上仙
若水老兄正之蒙清水芙蓉遠裏作此畵
二菱大人

Autumn

杞菊垂珠滴露红

把菊垂珠滴露紅
兩蛩相應語莎叢
嘉絲冒盡黃葵業
寂歷高花側晚風

37

*W*ith pearl-drops lingering in their
   pendent blooms,
Grow golden lilies, red chrysanthemums.
Conceal'd nearby, in sedgy marshland, live
A pair of crickets, spry and talkative.
Arachne from her self-spun endless sleaves
Has clothed in silk the yellow malva leaves.
The tall flowers, as evening claims her own,
Under the wind their lonely heads incline.

朱門巧夕沸歡聲
田舍黃昏靜掩扃
男解牽牛女能織
不須徼福渡河星

*I*n the rich house the girls laugh and sing:
The festival Begging Good Luck is in full
    swing.
At fall of dusk the simple cottager,
Seeing the night approach, makes fast his
    door.
Our women having Silver Weave in care,
And Heavenly Herd being the men's affair,
No need to pray those river-ferrying stars
With lovers' joys to load our household jars.

橋轟如蠶八化機
枝間垂蒲似叢衣
忽然悅作多花蝶
翅粉繞乾便學飛

39

The orange grub, which time must soon
    translate,
Like silkworm enters upon its middle state,
Between the boughs, enclosed in a cocoon
Of leaf-like tegument, to dangle down.
And now, shedding the husk, it blossoms
    forth
Into a brilliant many-colour'd moth,
Whose budded wings, bedew'd with natal
    spray,
She first unfolds, then stretches out to dry.

静看簷蛛結網低
無端妨礙小蟲飛
蜻蜓倒掛蜂兒窘
催唤山童為解圍

40

*H*ere Madam Spider spins and weaves
Her web under the low eaves,
Plotting to take and hold in snare
The wing'd unwary passenger.
A dragonfly and bees, in dire suspense,
Hang there for evidence:
Which sight so little pleases my old age,
I send my rustic boy to raise the siege.

要成穡事苦艱難　忍而媚風更怕寒
幾訴天公休撓剝　半償私債半輸官

41

*N*ow fields ready for scythe are all
   our care,
And heavy grows the burden of the year.
Afraid lest winter storms untimely come,
And cold weather deal the harvest doom,
We'll send a letter to the heavenly lord
Praying him not to plunder our small
      hoard:
For half the crop must go to pay our debts,
The other half in taxes to the state.

秋来久怕雨垂、甲

子無雲萬事宜穫

稻畢工随晾穀直

須晴刈入倉時

42

*A*utumn come, and *chia tzu* so near,
Mischance of rain is now our only fear.
But happy dawns the day: unclouded time
Enfolds ten thousand doings in one dream.
Harvest gather'd, we take the unthresh'd
    grain
And spread it in the sun,
Praying the weather may continue good
Until our barns receive the ripen'd food.

中秋無景屬潛夫
輝一色明有太湖身
外此天銀一色城中
有此月明無

43

A clear autumnal night! A full moon!
The solitary scene is all my own.
The moony water stretching wide and bare,
On idle oar I enter the tranced air.
Water and sky, suspending like a dream,
Contain me in a vast besilver'd room.
Who then would live in town,
Where such illumination is unknown?

新築場泥鏡面平

家家打稻趁霜晴

笑歌聲裏輕雷動

一夜連枷響到明

44

Through the new-built yard, smooth as
    looking-glass,
Group after group of busy workers pass:
For the threshing of rice-grain they come
    together,
Taking advantage of fine frosty weather.
Rustic voices, joking, singing, rumbling,
Are like a remote thunder's gentle
    grumbling;
And all night long, till the first glimmer of
    dawn,
The rhythmic beat of the flail goes on and
    on.

祖那滿載猴開倉

糕糕如珠白似霜不

惜兩鍾輪一斛舂

贏輝霰飽兒郎

45

*U*ntil the excisemen open their barn
    doors
To take of us these tributary stores,
Loaded with pearly grain as white as frost
Our waiting ships must lie along the coast.
Without complaint we render what is due:
Out of two *chung* we do not grudge one *hu*.
For still there's left to us, when all's done,
Some husky rice to feed the children on.

105

散粟瓶罌眇誦家天
教將醉作生涯不知
新滴堪蒭末今歲重
陽有菊花

46

*R*ich store of pulse and corn, this
thriving year,
Crams to the brim our jars of earthenware.
By heaven's gift of good fermentable grain
We tread already the royal way of wine,
Though hardly knowing, liquor still so new,
If yet to add our leaflings of bamboo.
And now the Day of Double Brightness
comes,
With autumn's festal flowers,
chrysanthemums.

細擣棖虀買鱠魚
西風吹上の腮鱸
雲鬆酥臘千絲縷
除卻松江到雾無

47

With onions finely minced, this mess
of fish
Makes quite a tolerable dish.
But in my heart I feel the west wind blow,
Luring from watery deeps the four-gill'd *lu*:
A thousand oily snow-white slips are laid
Once more before me, neatly filleted.
O fond pretence! Only in Pine River
Is that immortal fin seen to quiver!

新霜徹曉報秋深

染盡青林作頒林

惟有橘園風景異

碧叢叢裏萬黃金

48

*N*ightlong endures this unexpected
frost,
A sign that autumn nears her end at last:
The woods, where yesterday only greenness
was,
Wear now a richly-embroidered silken dress.
Here, in my orange-garden's secret air,
Another transformation is astir:
Hidden among these leaves of emerald
Ten thousand golden spheres are safe in
fold.

冬

日

Winter

斜 日 低 山 片 月 高

斜日低山片月高眠

徐行藥徑遶江郊

霜風搏盡千林葉

閒倚筇枝數鶴巢

49

Low lie the hills as day goes slowly down:
High above is a pale slice of moon.
Drowsy from sleep I swallow my due
    potion,
Then take a stroll to set my blood in
    motion.
Tall trees, assaulted by the frosty wind,
With twice ten thousand leaves scatter the
    ground.
Leaning upon my staff, I noddingly
Compute how many herons' nests there be.

117

炙背檐前日似烘
煖醺醺後困蒙蒙
過門走馬何官職
倒帽籠鞭戰北風

50

Like a man at his own hearth this elderly one
Under the eaves he stands, his back to the sun.
Warmth like wine, a glowing gradual bliss,
Blurs his sense with heavenly drowsiness.
Suddenly a horse goes galloping past the gate:
What man is the rider, and what his office of state,
Who, hat askew, clutching his reins, whipping his horse,
In face of the bleak north wind follows a struggling course?

屋上添高一把茅
蒼泥房壁似僧寮
泣教屋外陰風吼
卧聽籬頭響玉簫

51

Now add we to the roof another patch
Of dried rushes to reinforce the thatch;
Like monks' pavilions safe from winter's
harm,
With thicker clay-cast make our houses
warm.
So we be safe inside, and he without,
Let the wind roar at his pleasure and tear
about,
While we within enjoy the music he makes,
Playing his flute in the fence of bamboo-
stakes.

松節煙青當媽
籠凝炬如墨暗房
櫳晚來拭淨南窗
紙便覺斜陽倍紅

52

A pine-tree flare instead of a candle-
cage
Befits my rusticating age:
Like black ink the aroma drifting slow
Hangs in the air of room and portico.
When evening comes I approach the dark
pane
Of the south window and wipe its paper
clean:
The which no sooner done
Than instantly it fills with reddening sun.

乾高寅缺築牛官
芘酒豚蹄酹出勾
枯柞無瘟犢兒長
明年添種越城東

*H*ere, where the crust of the world
    cracks,
Under the constellation of the Ox
We raise to the earth-spirit our simple
    shrine,
Ritually offering leg of pork, and wine.
When bulls and cows from pestilence are
    free,
Calves wax fat and flourish stalwartly.
Next year we plan to extend our farm
    ground
Eastward, beyond the city's bound.

放船閒看雪山晴
風定奇寒晚更凝
坐聽一篙珠玉碎
不知湖面已成冰

54

Let the boat take me leisurely where
    it will,
So of these snow-bright slopes I have my
    fill.
The wind falls, is still. Cold and fine,
The evening air grows ever more crystalline.
The rhythmic pole makes music in my ears
Like breaking jade or shatter of pearly
    spheres:
By which I guess the water's shining face
Already wears a brittle sheet of ice.

撥雪挑來踏地菘味
如蜜藕更肥醲朱
門肉食無風味只作
尋常菜把供

55

Sweeping away the snow, we gather
   now
Cabbages of the sort called 'spreading low':
Like honey'd lotus-roots are they, for scent,
And in the mouth even more succulent.
At the grand house with the red-painted
   gate,
Where for unfastidious palates there's much
   to eat,
There they regard this heavenly vegetable
As merely another dish, and undelectable.

榾柮無煙雪夜長
地爐煨酒煖如湯
莫嗔老婦無盤飣
笑指灰中芋栗香

56

*T*hroughout the long, unending night of
   snow,
His knobs of smokeless charcoal burn and
   glow.
On earthen hearth he warms the wine,
   whose steam,
As night wears on, with fragrance fills the
   room.
'Don't blame old wife,' she says, 'for lack
   of care,
Because no dish of food she did prepare!'
And shows him, smiling, where, for his
   comfort's sake,
Taroes and chestnuts in the ashes bake.

煮酒春前臘後蒸

一年長饗甕頭清

塵居何似山居樂

秋米新東禁入城

57

*B*etween the feast of La and first of
spring
There's wine to make ready and set a-
simmering,
So by good luck we'll never lack to hear
The clink of brimming greentops all the
year.
You who live in the towns with noise and
smoke,
How are you better off than country folk,
Especially now, when new rules ordain
We send you not our luscious millet-grain?

黄紙蠲租白紙催

皂衣奔午下鄉束

長官頭腦冬烘甚

乞汝青錢買酒迴

58

A yellow tax-paper brings good luck
  your way.
Not so the white: that means you have to
  pay.
A smooth black-coated gentleman from
  town
Arrives one day at noon:
'How tiresome the caprices of the great!
My honour'd seniors, ministers of state
Whose ordinance one cannot but comply
  with,
Beg your green-insect money to buy wine
  with.'

135

探梅公子欵柴門枝

折枝南從東春色

見小桃紅似錦都

疑儂是武陵人

59

A well-born youth, in quest of
    blossoming plum,
To the faggot-door of my small cottage is
    come.
North and south the barren branches sway,
Still unaware that spring is on the way.
All of a sudden, turning his lordly head,
He sees a flowering peach-tree, damask red.
Celestial sight! It sets him wondering
Am I perhaps a native of Wu Ling?

村巷冬年見俗情
鄰翁講禮拜榮荊
長衫布縷如霜雪
云是家機自織成

60

*I*n village highways, when the year ends,
Each winter sees a festival of friends.
Good neighbours won't neglect, for
     anything,
The ritual of the mutual visiting.
In long, linen garments, white as snow,
From house to wooden house the old men
     go.
'Give you good den,' they'll say. ' 'Twas
     made at home,
This gown of mine: wove on our own
     loom.'

By Ts'ui Chi

Poem 3

The Festival of Purity and Brightness is a festival inspiring to poets. According to the old lunar calendar, it was either the fifth or the sixth day of the fourth moon, and thus it indicates the end of the spring season. This engenders in the people a sentiment of farewell to the best season of the year. For the Chinese summer is hot and unpleasant. The festival is celebrated by a ceremonial of picnicking outside the cities. People sojourn in the countryside with their families and friends. It is called 'The Tramping on the Green'. Family sepulchres are visited, and the dust wiped from the tombs, on which new earth is piled. Sacrifices are offered to the ancestral spirits. The day, as it appears in poetry, is often wet, with almond flowers blossoming and willow trees teeming with life in the rain.

Poem 4

'Faggots and Rushes' is also the name of a cheap wine. (*Chiu Shih*.)

Poem 4

The country inn is literally in Chinese 'a flag pavilion'. It is an officially managed house, selling wine:

> *The wine-flag towers from the willow trees, wafting in the breeze,*
> *A thatched house stands at the foot of the sloping hill.*

—as a poet sees it, this is a general picture of the ancient country inn.

Poem 5

It is an ancient Chinese custom to put money in the coffins of the dead, so that the ghosts may not be in want. As silk was at times used as currency, this was some-times buried too. About the fifth century, the Marquis Tung-hun of Ch'i used paper money instead of silk. The burning of the paper money at the graveside is a token of its being given to the dead.

Poem 7

'Salad Festival' of the 'Cold Meal' day occurs 106 days after the Winter Solstice. The legend runs that when the young Prince Chung-erh of Tsin was in exile, his loyal friends followed him abroad through difficult years. The prince returned to his own country and became the powerful duke, the Civilized. He rewarded all his friends except one Chieh T'ui, the greatest friend of all. Without complaining, Chieh T'ui escaped to the mountains, away from the knowledge of society, and lived as a hermit. Later, when the duke came to remember him and became ashamed of his own ingratitude, he searched the mountain, and endeavoured to scorch the obstinate hermit out of his shelter. But Chieh T'ui had now made up his mind to refuse any reward, and as the flames spread, he remained where he was and was burnt to death. This tragic end so saddened the hearts of the gods, that they loathed the sight of fire from that day. In the district of Tsin a custom later developed that no fires must be built on that day. The oven and hearth in the kitchen must remain cold, and only salad must be eaten. In poetry it often appears to be a rainy day, a haze covering the willow trees on the river banks.

Poem 7

Ling Yen, the 'Divine Cliff', is to the west of Soochow. There are on the cliffs the remains of the palaces of the beautiful Queen Hsi Shih, one of which was her 'Terrace of the Lute'.

Hu Ch'iu, the 'Tiger's Slope', is sometimes called Hai Yung Shan—'The Hill of the Rising Sea'. Standing to the northwest of the city of Soochow, it is famous for its beauty. Three days after the burial of an ancient prince at the spot, according to the legends, a white tiger appeared and squatted on the top of his sepulchre. Hence the derivation of the name Tiger's Slope.

Poem 13

Heng Tang is a famous lake, south-west of Soochow. To the north was the Maple Bridge, and to the south the Lake of Dimple. On the shores was a town called Heng Tang, the girls of which town are famous for their beauty.

Poem 14

The season of the 'Yellowing Plum' is marked by rainy weather. This period occurs about the end of the fourth moon of the year in the Soochow district, and when moisture is plentiful in the air the mellowing plum fruits turn gold-coloured and fall.

Poem 16

Shang Ch'ih was the first *'ch'ih'* day in the first decade of the third moon (cf. Poem 42, Note). On this day people went to bathe in eastward-flowing streams in order to get rid of any ill luck, which was then carried away to the eastern seas by the flowing water. The day was later on fixed as the third of the month.

Poem 23

This fish is sometimes called the 'stone-headed' because of the hard bone which is in its head. Its scientific name is perhaps *Sciaena schlegeli*.

Poem 32

It was the ancient tradition to plant three elm trees outside the emperor's court. These marked the position facing which three of the emperor's ministers, with the equivalent rank of 'duke', stood. Hence the 'three trees' symbolized high rank in the court.

Poem 36

'The art of being dull of sense' is to play foolish and deaf, when required; there is a Chinese saying:

Unless you are foolish and deaf,
You cannot become a good parent-in-law.

A story is told of a haunted house wherein dwelt a fierce demon, which transformed itself into horrible beings in order to frighten its victim to death. Sometimes, however, it changed into a beautiful woman, and hurt the man who fell in love with 'her'. An old monk, blind and deaf, happened to lodge in the same house and sat up all night alone, meditating. The demon came and tried to tempt or frighten him, but with no success. The monk could neither hear nor see, and was quite ignorant of its existence. The demon sighed and withdrew, and, perhaps ashamed of itself, vanished for ever.

Poem 38

The granddaughter of the Emperor of the Heavens was in love with the Herd of the Sky. This love affair provoked the Emperor to fury, and he decided that the young couple must be separated by the Silver River (the Milky Way), across which they

147

could see one another, but could not hear one another speak, nor could they meet. At her stern grandfather's order, the young princess was told to weave a damask which could never be woven. This was the rainbow-like tatters of cloud which appear in the golden dusk. The princess's love-sickness therefore never ceased. But after a long time her royal grandfather began to pity her, and allowed her to meet the Herd on the other side of the River once a year on the seventh day of the seventh moon. On that evening the Divine Magpies would fly in a chain over the river and make a bridge for the girl to cross. The next day the white magpies disappeared from the sky, and we find the Weaving Girl back at her work beyond the reach of the Herd.

This is only a story of the stars, but down in our mundane world this is the Love Festival, which is called 'The Night of Begging Good Luck' (*ch'iao hsi*), or— because *chi* (begging) can also mean seven —'The Night of Seven Good Lucks'. In the noontime Chinese girls and women play a game of divination: they put coloured silk through the 'seven holes' of a specially made needle and throw this on a bowl of water placed in the sun. 'The needle stays afloat' and the lady looks at the shadow to see the omen, which appears in various forms—clouds, flowers, animals, shoes, scissors, etc. These pictures determine the future of the questioner's love affair.

Poem 39

When the poet mentions the transforming orange grub, he probably alludes to the philosophy of the existence of human beings. How transient and unreal is life! One can find noble pleasure in an orange as much as in society and the court. The book *Yu Kuai Lu* describes the story of the 'old men in the orange' of the Pa-Ch'iung orchard. There grew on one tree a large orange like an earthen jar. Somebody cut it open and found, seated inside, two old men playing chess. They told their discoverer that in the orange it was as pleasant as on the hermit's hills of Shang Shan. One thing they regretted about their orange abode was that whilst the hermit's hill was deep-rooted in the earth, the world inside the orange was so unstable that it could be removed from its stalk at any time.

Poem 42

The Chinese counted the days in the month by a combined system of two branches of starry names, one containing ten names beginning with the word *chia*, and the other twelve names beginning with *tzu*. When interpolated, these compose sixty different names. *Chia-tzu* is the first day of a unit-cycle.

Poem 43

The Chinese used a lunar calendar, and the night of the fifteenth of the eighth moon, when the moon becomes full, is called the Middle Autumn Festival. The ancient queen Ch'ang O, wife of the Great Archer, according to legend, was entrusted by her husband with the care of some elixir, the eater of which would become immortalized. The queen swallowed the medicine herself, and acquired the art of flying into the air. But her husband chased after her, and she fled to the Heavenly World and became the Goddess of the Moon. This new rank did not bring her much pleasure, for looking down at the noisy world, where romances occur endlessly, she became love-sick and lonely:

Ch'ang O must regret that she has swal-lowed the elixir:
Night after night the sea is blue, the sky emerald, and her lonely heart is never consoled.

So sings the poet Li Shang-yin.

Poem 46

The Festival of Double Brightness is, by the Chinese calendar, the ninth day of the ninth moon—the number nine is a masculine number and the symbol of 'brightness', while number six is 'shadowy' and feminine. The chrysanthemum is in full bloom at this season, and it is the custom to admire this flower with a feast of wine and crabs. The poet Tao Ch'ien was a great lover of this flower, and the festival also preserves the poet's memory. According to the book *Hsu Ch'i Hsieh Chi*, a gentleman named Huan was the friend of a magician, who warned him that calamity of the epidemic kind would spread and ruin the

151

town, but if Huan would go with his family to some mountain on the ninth day of the ninth moon, each wearing a bag of stuffed *chu yü* grass, and drink wine spiced with chrysanthemum petals, their lives could be saved. This they did, and when they returned home in the evening, they found the dead bodies of chickens, dogs and sheep strewn on the ground. A custom was developed on the strength of this legend. On that day of every year people would climb up mountains, wearing the *chu yü* grass. Each member of the family was given a spike of grass, and anyone absent from the gathering would be remembered by the rest of the family. Abroad, the traveller would feel homesick on this day, as the poet says:

> *In my mind's eye, I see my brothers climbing the mountains;*
> *While they distribute the* chu yü *flowers, they find one of their beloved ones absent.*

Poem 47

The *lu* fish is a Chinese perch. Usually it has two gills, but the fish living in the Pine

River, west of a town of that name to the east of Soochow, has four and is particularly delicious. The poet Su Shih admires it in his famous poem 'The Red Cliff'. The fish is best cooked with a green vegetable called *hsun ts'ai*. In the third century a poet, Chang Han, from Soochow travelled to the north, and served in the court of the prince Ch'i. But Chang Han soon grew weary of politics, in which he had become involved, and he felt very homesick when the golden wind of autumn blew. He was suddenly seized with a longing desire to have a dinner in his home town, of the *hsun ts'ai* with the four-gilled perch. 'Oh, one should live to please oneself. What is the use of wealth and power which do not please me?' he sighed, and on that same day he resigned his post and drove home in a light chariot. A few months after he had gone, the prince's influence collapsed and he was assassinated. The poet is praised not only for his noble taste, but also for his political foresight. '*Hsun ts'ai* and four-gilled perch' is in the Chinese dictionary a rhetorical term expressing a homesick feeling.

Poem 57

Greentops, literally: 'green at the top of the wine-jar'. The reference is to newly made wine which is yet mellow enough for drinking. An alternative phrase, used by a T'ang poet, was 'Spring at the top of the wine-jar'.

Poem 58

Owing to the metallic alloys in it, Chinese coin looked green, and was known as the 'green coin'. The greenness, however, is also associated with the legend of an insect called the green *fu*. The parental instinct of this insect is so strong that profiteers made use of it. Some mother-insects were killed and their blood smeared on eighty-one (a magic number) coins, also some children-insects were killed and their blood smeared on another eighty-one coins; these were henceforth called mother-money and children-money. These were put together in a jar, and buried 'at the foot of the eastern wall' for three days, until the affection grew to such an extent that they were inseparable from one another. Either the mother-money was used to keep the children-money in safety, or the reverse. In both cases the money paid out would come back to the user voluntarily.

Poem 59

A native of Wu Ling. Once during the Tai Yuan period of the Tsin dynasty, writes the poet Tao Chi'en, a certain fisherman from Wu Ling lost his way and came to a stream. Along the banks of the stream grew innumerable peach trees which were in full bloom. Attracted by their beauty, the fisherman pursued his way among the flowers, and came to a small crack in the mountain. He crept in. The path was extremely narrow at first, then it opened out and the fisherman found himself standing before a populated valley. The residents looked very gay and very kind. All of them seemed to work in the fields, and all were well-to-do. They invited the fisherman to their homes, and entertained him with rice and chicken. They told him that their ancestors had moved into this valley during the disturbing years at the end of the Ch'in dynasty, nearly six centuries ago, and they had never known the political upheavals which had taken place outside. They were contented and happy, and made the fisherman promise never to reveal their existence to the world. But the fisherman could not keep his word: when he returned from the valley he went to tell the mayor, who instantly sent men in search of the place. Fortunately, the fisherman had lost his own tracks; the mayor died soon after; and the secret remained undiscovered.